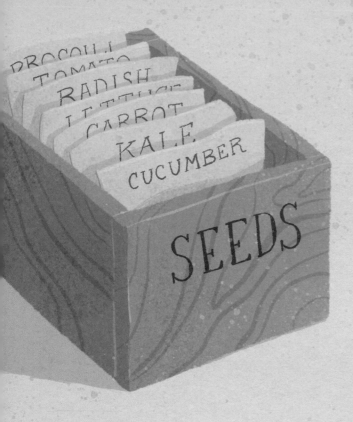

To my wonderful, pie-loving family
—SH

For Mom and Dad, my two favorite gardeners
—Chamisa

SLEEPING BEAR PRESS™

2395 South Huron Parkway, Suite 200, Ann Arbor, MI 48104
www.sleepingbearpress.com • © Sleeping Bear Press
Manufactured in China.
ISBN: 978-1-53411-184-4
10 9 8 7 6 5 4 3 2 1
Names: Heavenrich, Sue, author. | Kellogg, Chamisa, illustrator.
Title: The pie that Molly grew / Sue Heavenrich ; pictures by Chamisa Kellogg.
Description: Ann Arbor, MI : Sleeping Bear Press, 2023. | Audience: Ages 4-8. | Audience: Grades 2-3. | Summary: Using "The House That Jack
Built" rhyme scheme, a young girl plants a seed and follows its journey from sprout to vine to the final fruit which she then uses to bake a
pie. Includes information on pumpkins and a pumpkin pie recipe. Identifiers: LCCN 2023000849 | ISBN 9781534111844 (hardcover)
Subjects: CYAC: Stories in rhyme. | Pastry--Fiction. | Pumpkin--Fiction. | Gardens--Fiction. | LCGFT: Stories in rhyme. | Picture books.
Classification: LCC PZ8.3.H3838 Pi 2023 | DDC [E]--dc23 | LC record available at https://lccn.loc.gov/2023000849
Photo Credits: Squash Bee: Claire Anna Jones/Shutterstock.com; Bumble Bee: Paul Reeves Photograph/Shutterstock.com; Honey Bee: TippaPatt/Shutterstock.com;
Sweat Bee: Barbara Storms/Shutterstock.com; Long Horned Bee: Jennifer Bosvert/Shutterstock.com; Carpenter bee: samray/Shutterstock.com

The Pie That Molly grew

Sue Heavenrich 🌱 Pictures by Chamisa Kellogg

PUBLISHED BY SLEEPING BEAR PRESS™

This is the seed
that Molly sowed.

This is the **Sprout** that pushed through the earth to grow from the seed that Molly sowed.

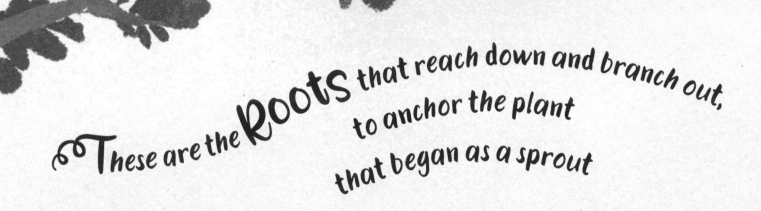

These are the **Roots** that reach down and branch out,
to anchor the plant
that began as a sprout

to grow from the seed that Molly sowed.

These are the LEaVES as big as your head,
turning sunlight to food wherever they spread
to store in the roots that reach down and branch out,

to anchor the plant

that began as a sprout

to grow from the seed that Molly sowed.

This is the **Vine** that rambles and grows,
a spiky green lifeline through which water flows
from the roots to the leaves as big as your head,
turning sunlight to food wherever they spread

then back to the roots that reach down and branch out,
to anchor the plant
that began as a sprout
to grow from the seed that Molly sowed.

These are the BLOSSOMS yellow and bold,
producers of pollen more precious than gold.
They bloom on the vine that never stops growing,
a spiky green lifeline that keeps water flowing
from the roots to the leaves as big as your head,

turning sunlight to food wherever they spread
then back to the roots that reach down and branch out,
to anchor the plant
that began as a sprout
to grow from the seed that Molly sowed.

These are the **BEES** that carry the pollen
from flower to flower
till petals have fallen,
revealing small fruits on the vine green and strong
that serves as a lifeline to move things along—

from the leaves to the fruits to the roots that branch out,
to anchor the plant
that began as a sprout
to grow from the seed that Molly sowed.

This is the **PUMPKIN** ripe and round
that came from a seed poked into the ground,
nurtured from sprout and a deep-spreading root
shaded by leaves as it grew to a fruit

that got sliced and seasoned and baked in a pan
and left on the table till feasting began.

These are the PEOPLE all gathered in thanks
for the earth and the sun,
for the rain the plant drank,

for the seed and the sprout,
for the vine and the leaves,
for the flowers that nourished the hardworking bees,

and the wonderful

pie that Molly made.

American pie

There are more than 45 kinds of pumpkins. They come in many colors—red, gold, blue, white—but most are orange. The earliest pumpkins were grown by Native Americans more than 6,000 years ago.

While it's true that the Pilgrims baked pumpkin for their first Thanksgiving, they didn't make pie. But you can! And like Molly, you can grow your own pie pumpkins. All you need is sunshine, seeds, and a place to plant them. You also need room for their vines to spread out.

Before planting, mix a bit of compost (well-rotted leaves or manure) into the soil. This provides food for the pumpkin plants. Sow four or five seeds in an area the size of a large pizza. When seedlings are about six inches tall, cut out the two smallest. The plants left in the garden will grow stronger. If you start a pumpkin inside, you can plant it outside in a garden or large pot. Cover bare soil with a layer of straw or dried grass and leaves to keep weeds from growing. This also helps keep the soil from drying out, and it will remind you to not plant other things there.

After a few weeks you'll see flowers. When pumpkins start forming, they look like tiny green balls below the flower.

Pumpkins are ripe when they are a deep orange color. They are ready to pick when you can't poke your fingernail through the skin. It takes a sharp knife to cut through thick pumpkin stems, so ask an adult to help cut your pumpkin from the vine. Leave a couple inches of stem attached to the fruit. Then wipe off the dirt and store your pumpkin in a cool, dry area until you're ready to make pie.

How to Turn a Pumpkin into Pie
(Be sure to have a grown-up help you)

1. Roast the pumpkin. Turn the oven to 350 degrees F and cut a ripe pumpkin in half. Hint: it's easier to cut it from stem to bottom.

2. Scoop out the seeds and stringy stuff inside.

3. Place the pumpkin halves, open side down, in a large baking dish. Add about one-half inch of water and put it in the oven for about 45 minutes. It's done when you can poke a fork through the skin.

4. After the pumpkin cools, scrape the cooked fruit into a bowl and mash it up. A potato masher is perfect for this job.

When you're ready to make the pie...

Turn the oven to 425 degrees F.

Make a pie crust or use a ready-made crust.

To make the filling, mix all of these ingredients in a large bowl:

- 2 cups mashed pumpkin
- 1 13-ounce can evaporated milk
- 2 eggs
- ½ cup brown sugar
- ½ cup granulated sugar
- 1 ½ teaspoons cinnamon
- ½ teaspoon each of ground ginger, nutmeg, allspice, and cloves

Put the pie tin on the oven rack and pour the pumpkin mixture into the pie crust. It gets a bit splashy, so pour carefully, and ease the rack back into place. Bake at 425 degrees F for 15 minutes. Then turn down the heat to 350 and bake another 35 minutes or more. When the filling is set, the pie is done. To test: put in a clean knife. If it comes out gloppy, bake the pie longer.

No Bees, No Pie

Pumpkin plants produce male flowers and female flowers. They depend on bees to move the pollen from the male flower to the female flower. Once female flowers have pollen, they can grow into pumpkins.

The bees that carry pollen come in all sizes, from big fuzzy bumblebees to shiny emerald sweat bees. Without bees, we'd have no pie.

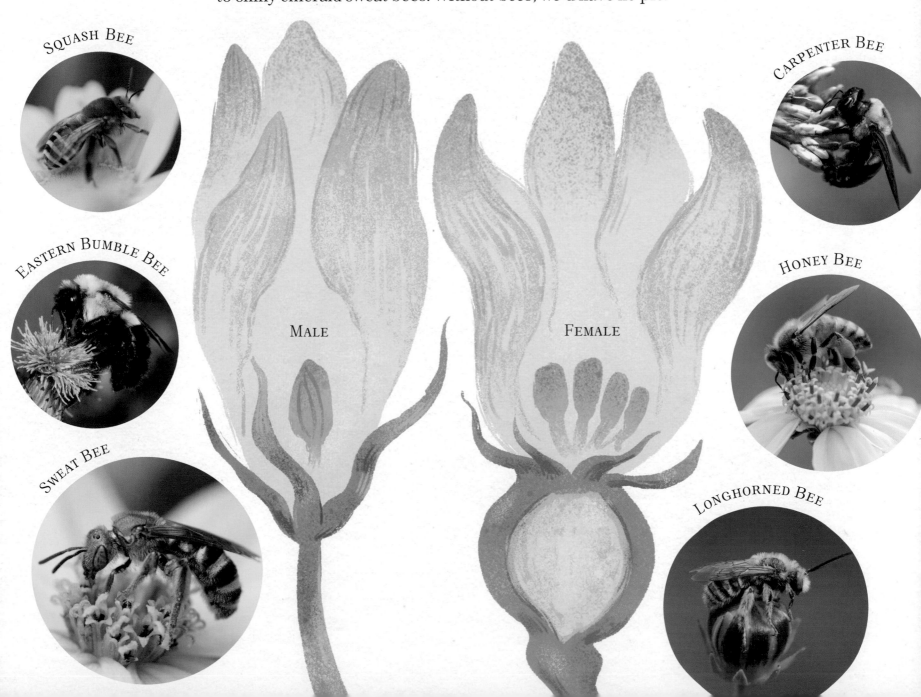

SQUASH BEE

CARPENTER BEE

EASTERN BUMBLE BEE

HONEY BEE

MALE

FEMALE

SWEAT BEE

LONGHORNED BEE